Go to godsfavoredfive.com and join our FREE email list for access to audio readings of our books and access to additional resources to enhance your child's learning.

You can also sign up for the Learning With Gabriel and Ellise Bookclub! Come learn with us!

Copyright©2022 by Gabriel Cazeau, Ellise Cazeau, Joni Cazeau All rights reserved.

ISBN: 978-1-955684-08-8

Published by God's Favored Five https://godsfavoredfive.com

Illustrated by: Jean Cazeau

Translated by: Enante Bourdeau, Moise Bourdeau

GOD'S FAVORED FIVE

LEARNING WITH GABRIEL AND ELLISE

ENGLISH & FRENCH

Illustrated By Jean Cazeau

Translated by: Enante Bourdeau, Moise Bourdeau

Hi! My name is Gabriel.
Salut! Je m'appelle Gabriel.

This is my sister, Ellise.
C'est ma sœur, Ellise.

Nous aimons les couleurs.

Blue
Bleu

The sky is blue
Le ciel est bleu.

Red

Rouge.

This truck is red.
Ce camion est rouge.

Green
Vert/Verte

The grass is green.
L'herbe est verte.

Orange
Orange

An orange is orange.
Une orange est orange.

Purple
Mauve

The flower is purple.
La fleur est mauve.

Brown.
Marron.

The block is brown.
Le bloc est marron.

White.
Blanc/Blanche.

The church is white.
L'église est blanche.

Black.
Noir.

The horse is black.
Le cheval est noir.

Reinforce your learning at Godsfavoredfive.com

and

Our Learning with Gabriel and Ellise Youtube channel

CPSIA information can be obtained
at www.ICGtesting.com
Printed in the USA
LVHW070512090622
720761LV00001B/18